ERICH PETER NEUMANN / ELISABETH NOELLE

STATISTICS
ON
ADENAUER

PORTRAIT OF A STATESMAN

Ⴘ

VERLAG FÜR DEMOSKOPIE

English, revived edition. Title of the German edition: „Umfragen über Adenauer. Ein Porträt in Zahlen." 1961. English translation by John Fosberry.

Set and printed in Germany by: Kölnische Verlagsdruckerei GmbH, Köln

CONTENTS

Foreword   VII

Personalia   I   3

Position   II   17

Approval, Criticism   III   33

Rivals and Successors   IV   59

President or Chancellor?   V   81

International Relations   VI   107

The Politician   VII   119

The Great Name   VIII   135

Appendix   151

FOREWORD

Historians regularly find themselves in an awkward position when they are called upon to depict the impact of an important person on his surroundings. The material with which they have to make do up to about the end of the 18th century is not, in fact, very revealing. Frequently the sources are dubious; it is all a matter of interpretation. Then the press furnished the historians with new information facilities. With respect to reliability, however, not very much was gained. Their support for one party usually was more important to the papers than an objective report.

With the development of photography and film, the era of technical documentation began. Records and magnetic tapes enhanced the optical perfection by means of sound recordings. How gripping were the early stages of this development, daguerreotypes of Napoleon III, moving pictures with the blurred features of Tsar Nikolaus, Wilson's voice on the gramophone. Nowadays, every college is equipped with the necessary apparatus to present personalities and events of the last few decades in picture and sound. None of the audiences of these marvellous presentations will think of their inventors, such as Edison or Lumière.

For the chroniclers, the actions of historic figures are more important than contemporary conceptions of them. The public opinion they provoked at their time is not decisive for the picture that is handed down to posterity. Their actions, whether barbaric or benevolent, form the basis for their judgement — not sympathy or antipathy.

The forces with the help of which society brings about its eternal changes would become more subtly clear to the analyst who evaluates historic events, if we knew with certainty to what degree the public in the various ages played a part in the vagaries of politics.

Indubitably, general interest in the psychological and sociological causes of events and conditions is still growing. In the same way, the demand for a refinement of research methods is becoming ever greater. Advances in this direction can only be achieved gradually, step by step. This book is intended to provide a slight impetus towards progress along this road. Therefore others will follow this example — not today, but perhaps the day after tomorrow.

★ ★

The fact that this book aims at presenting the personality of Konrad Adenauer, the German Federal Chancellor, in figures is in itself a matter of no real importance. The prime consideration is the statistical portrait of a statesman — any statesman — of this era. Any man who, in times to come, ever holds a similarly exposed political position for such a long period, will be observed just as systematically; not only in democratic Germany, but in most countries of the free world. It would be just as possible to publish statistical portraits of Roosevelt, Truman and Eisenhower — based on poll results in the U.S.A. — as we are now doing in the case of Adenauer. But a start had to be made somewhere.

The German Institut für Demoskopie at Allensbach has been following Adenauer's political career since 1949 with statistically representative polls. Month after month, samples comprising 2,000 people were induced to air their opinion on the Chancellor's policies. Inspired partly by daily events and partly by their penchant for research, the Institute staff also carried out other investigations into the qualities, intentions and actions of the Federal Chancellor. This publication contains a selection of the material collected.

* *

Hence it is a statistical record of public opinion in the German Federal Republic regarding Konrad Adenauer. But is it of any use to evaluate in tables the vacillating, changing, ever varying opinion of a public of which frequently too much is expected? Is it of any profit to the political and the scientific field?

The reader will either hold this publication to be an arid desert, or a glimpse of all the treasures in Ali Baba's cave. Concentration is a vital precondition for understanding the language of the tables, and great objectivity and creative imagination is indispensable to evaluate them. They shed bright, uncompromising light on a politician of international rank. It is to be hoped that it will lead to a better understanding of the Adenauer era, and not only by our successors.

Allensbach am Bodensee, Spring 1962

The Publishers

PERSONALIA

I

How does the German public see Adenauer? There have been enough opportunities to get to know him; his picture in papers and magazines, his voice over the radio, his aura through the intimate medium of television. Nearly all the inhabitants of the Federal Republic of Germany have a clear conception of his face and his voice. But strict matter-of-factness, and sometimes even uneasy coolness determine the general atmosphere of this relationship. Unchanging over the course of the years, a quite substantial group of approximately 20 per cent says they do not like his face. He is constantly the target of some antipathy and biting criticism. However, only comparisons on the same methodological level could reveal whether the public reacts similarly to other politicians, who hold a high government post for a long time — or whether Adenauer's character and comportment substantially influence that atmosphere.

No matter how severely he has been, and still is, dealt with by public opinion, one trait arouses the sympathies of the public: his weakness for roses is very popular.

A clever, diplomatically gifted and, above all, tough politician, who is pious, industrious, conscientious — that is the image reflected in public opinion. It is characteristic of the scepticism with which he is regarded that only 10 per cent consider him a genius, and again only 10 per cent think him kind-hearted. The thesis that he satisfies the father-complex of the German people has little to justify it. But he possesses that degree of natural authority, which the Germans tend to consider a special merit.

Question: "Do you know what Adenauer looks like; have you ever seen a picture of him?"

A	1953 July	1957 July
	%	%
Yes, I know	94	98
No, I don't know	6	2
Total	100	100

Question put to persons who know what Adenauer looks like and have seen a picture of him: "If you did not know who he is and saw a picture of him somewhere, would you like his face or not?"

	1953 July	1957 July
	%	%
Like	38	36
Dislike	22	27
Undecided, indifferent	34	35
Remainder not questioned	6	2
Total	100	100

Question: "Do you think that pictures of Adenauer always show him younger than he really is, or don't you believe that?"

	Don't believe it	Believe so	Some- times	Un- decided	Total
	%	%	%	%	%
Total population	66	15	8	11	= 100
Men	66	18	8	8	= 100
Women	66	13	7	14	= 100
CDU/CSU supporters .	76	13	6	5	= 100
SPD supporters	62	25	6	7	= 100

Question: "When you see Adenauer in pictures, do you have the impression that he is still capable of doing a great deal, or does he look too old?"

February 1957

	Can still do a great deal	Too old	Undecided	Total
	%	%	%	%
Total population	48	29	23	= 100
Men	49	31	20	= 100
Women	47	27	26	= 100
CDU/CSU supporters	72	14	14	= 100
SPD supporters	26	57	17	= 100

Question: "As far as you know, was Adenauer in Germany during the Hitler period, or was he abroad?"

April 1956

	In Germany %	Abroad %	Dont' know %	Total %
Total population	39	10	51	= 100
Men	47	13	40	= 100
Women.	31	9	60	= 100
Primary school	32	11	57	= 100
Secondary school.	63	9	28	= 100
CDU/CSU supporters . . .	46	7	47	= 100
SPD supporters	41	13	46	= 100
FDP/DVP supporters	52	18	30	= 100

Question: "As far as you know, was Adenauer in prison or a concentration camp during the Hitler period?"

April 1956

	In prison	In a concentration camp	Was not imprisoned	Don't know	Total
	%	%	%	%	%
Total population	17	13	13	60	= 103
Men	19	16	18	50	= 103
Women.	15	11	8	69	= 103
Primary school	15	12	10	66	= 103
Secondary school	25	18	21	41	= 105
CDU/CSU supporters . .	21	15	8	60	= 104
SPD supporters	16	13	14	59	= 102
FDP/DVP supporters . . .	26	20	18	39	= 103

Question: "Do you happen to know how old Adenauer is?" (If un-
known: "What would you imagine? About how old do you think?")

	1953 March	1957 February
	%	%
Correct answer	23	43
Age underestimated	65	38
Age overestimated	10	16
Don't know	2	3
Total	100	100

Question: "In Bonn it is sometimes important whether a politician
is Catholic or Evangelical. We would therefore like to find out how
many people know what politicians are Catholic or Protestant."

May 1959

	Total popu- lation	Men	Women	Supporters: CDU/ CSU	SPD	FDP/ DVP
	%	%	%	%	%	%
Konrad Adenauer is:						
Catholic	91	92	89	95	93	98
Protestant	1	×	1	1	1	×
Neither	×	×	×	×	×	×
Don't know	7	7	9	3	6	2
Konrad Adenauer unknown	1	1	1	1	×	×
Total	100	100	100	100	100	100

Question: "What do you think: How many hours does Adenauer work daily; what would you estimate?"

January 1957

	Total popu- lation	Men	Women	Prima- ry school	Secon- dary school	Supporters: CDU/ CSU	SPD	FDP/ DVP
	%	%	%	%	%	%	%	%
Up to 8 hours . .	23	23	23	23	21	17	32	29
9 hours . .	4	4	4	4	5	6	4	4
10 hours . .	13	16	12	14	14	18	13	20
11 hours . .	5	5	4	4	7	7	3	5
12 hours . .	8	8	7	6	11	10	7	8
More than 12 hours . .	9	10	8	8	14	15	6	10
Don't know	38	34	42	41	28	27	35	24
Total	100	100	100	100	100	100	100	100

Question: "What do you think Adenauer does in his spare time?"

September 1955

	Total popu-lation	Men	Women	Agri-culture	Wor-kers	Salaried employees, civil ser-vants	Indepen-dent trades and professions
	%	%	%	%	%	%	%
Rose growing, work in garden .	29	26	30	18	22	42	42
Rests, takes it easy . .	15	14	16	17	16	12	15
Reading	11	12	11	10	10	14	14
Walking	10	9	11	10	11	10	6
Visits his children, devotes himself to family. . . .	7	6	7	6	6	9	6
Sleeps	3	2	4	4	3	3	3
Prays, goes to church .	2	2	3	3	2	2	2
Other answers .	12	13	11	11	12	13	11
Has no spare time at all . . .	4	4	3	2	4	4	5
Don't know, don't care . . .	27	29	25	34	31	18	18
Total	120	117	121	115	117	127	122

Question: "How high do you estimate Adenauer's monthly salary? His personal salary — not allowances for representative purposes?"

	1952 May	1953 April
	%	%
Less than DM 2,000	20	23
DM 2,000 to 3,000	20	20
DM 3,000 to 5,000	23	24
DM 5,000 to 10,000	18	18
DM 10,000 and more	16	11
Don't know.	3	4
Total	100	100

Question: "And how much would you consider appropriate?"

	1952 May	1953 April
	%	%
Less than DM 2,000	57	50
DM 2,000 to 3,000	18	20
DM 3,000 to 5,000	10	13
DM 5,000 to 10,000	6	7
DM 10,000 and more	5	3
Don't know.	4	7
Total	100	100

Question: "What do you like most about Adenauer?"

November 1951

	Total popu- lation	Men	Women	Supporters: CDU/ CSU	SPD	FDP/ DVP
	%	%	%	%	%	%
Negotiating skill (diplomatic, adroit, quick-witted, gets best possible results)	9	13	6	17	9	17
Energy (will-power, tenacity, drive, endurance, activity) . .	9	11	7	17	8	13
Well-balanced personality, calmness (prudent, modest, wise)	4	5	4	7	2	11
Intelligence, clear judgment (straightforward line, long-term policy)	4	6	2	8	1	8
Upright character (backbone, fearless, courageous)	3	4	2	7	3	3
Effective appearance (outward appearance, man-of-the-world confidence, etc.)	2	1	2	2	2	1
Other traits	4	5	4	4	4	6
Absolutely nothing (and clearly negative traits and ironic remarks — e. g. "his frock-coat", "his obedience to the Allies")	24	30	18	7	39	17
Don't know, no answer . .	41	25	55	31	32	24
Total	100	100	100	100	100	100

Question: "Which of the following characteristics, in your opinion, is descriptive of Adenauer?"

	1955 January	1956 December	1958 October	1959 November
	%	%	%	%
Clever	57	55	55	44
Diplomatic	55	54	54	43
Persistent, tough	51	51	49	47
Industrious	43	44	40	32
Pious	42	53	48	38
Purposeful	42	41	41	35
Cultured	42	45	39	34
Ambitious	36	40	38	41
Conscientious	35	38	35	31
Likeable	30	27	31	22
Cunning, wily	30	35	37	35
Circumspect	21	24	22	16
Amiable	21	21	21	15
Obstinate	20	30	27	33
Unassuming	19	18	17	15
Upright	15	14	13	10
Relentless	15	24	23	25
Tyrannical	13	19	16	23
Kind-hearted	11	11	11	9
Unpleasant	10	9	9	10
Inexorable	9	12	12	10
Genius	9	10	12	9
Cold	8	10	8	9
Egoistic	6	8	8	11
False	5	4	3	4
Conscienceless	4	4	4	3
Domineering	4	4	5	5
Brusque, uncivil	3	5	5	4
Malicious	2	4	4	4
No statement, don't know . .	11	11	9	15
Total	669	725	696	632

Question: "When people say that Adenauer always uses every means to try to get his own way — do you think it is a point in his favour, or against him?"

March 1956

	Against him	In his favour	Undecided, don't know	Total
	%	%	%	%
Total population	36	35	29	= 100
Men	46	38	16	= 100
Women.	29	32	39	= 100
CDU/CSU supporters	20	55	25	= 100
SPD supporters	60	27	13	= 100
FDP/DVP supporters	52	33	15	= 100

Question put to persons of 21 and over: "Which of the leading politicians do you think has the best sense of humour?" (L)

February 1962

	Total population	Men	Women	Supporters: CDU/ CSU	SPD	FDP/ DVP
	%	%	%	%	%	%
Theodor Heuss . . .	50	54	48	46	56	79
Adenauer	20	22	18	30	13	13
Ludwig Erhard . . .	6	7	6	7	8	8
Willy Brandt	4	4	4	3	6	5
Krushchev	4	6	3	3	5	5
Strauss	3	5	2	5	2	5
Heinrich Lübke . . .	2	1	2	2	2	×
Kennedy	2	2	2	2	2	×
Macmillan	1	1	1	1	2	×
Nasser	×	×	×	×	×	×
de Gaulle	×	×	×	×	×	×
Ulbricht	×	×	×	×	×	×
No answer	24	17	29	20	19	13
Total	116	119	115	119	115	128

POSITION

II

All efforts to cast doubts on Adenauer's good intentions and his personal integrity have been set at nought by the public's resistance. Soon after his first election to the position of head of the government, the majority of the population of western Germany was convinced that he wanted the "best" for his country. After his first re-election to the same office, a relative majority confirmed that he made "equal efforts for all strata of the public" — at that time a very affirmative attitude which revealed almost kind feelings.

Question: "It is general knowledge that Adenauer and Schumacher (at this time the leader of the Social Democrats) almost never agree. Do you think it is a bad thing that Adenauer and Schumacher mostly hold different opinions?"

April 1951

	Is not bad %	Is bad %	Don't know %	Total %
Total population	52	22	26	= 100
Men	65	23	12	= 100
Women	42	21	37	= 100
Under 30 years old	53	21	26	= 100
30—44	55	21	24	= 100
45—59	51	23	26	= 100
60 and over	47	23	30	= 100
Primary school	48	22	30	= 100
Secondary school	63	23	14	= 100
Secondary school graduates ("Abitur")	77	19	4	= 100
Less than DM 100 monthly income	38	24	38	= 100
DM 100—249	53	22	25	= 100
DM 250—400	60	21	19	= 100
Over DM 400	60	23	17	= 100
North Germany	51	25	24	= 100
West Germany.	55	21	24	= 100
South Germany	51	21	28	= 100
West Berlin	52	21	27	= 100
CDU/CSU supporters	47	30	23	= 100
SPD supporters	62	23	15	= 100
FDP/DVP supporters	68	20	12	= 100
KPD supporters	65	13	22	= 100
BP supporters	46	29	25	= 100
DP supporters	60	18	22	= 100
BHE supporters	59	25	16	= 100

Question: "It is general knowledge that Adenauer and Ollenhauer (at this time the Social Democratic leader) almost never agree. Do you think it is a bad thing that Adenauer and Ollenhauer mostly hold different opinions?"

	1955 *May*	*1956* *June*
	%	%
Is not bad.	54	57
Is bad	27	20
Don't know	19	23
Total	100	100

Question: "Do you think that Adenauer primarily wants the best for Germany, or has he other interests that are more important to him?"

August 1953

A	Wants the best %	Has other interests %	Don't know %	Total %
Total population	66	10	24	= 100
Men	67	14	19	= 100
Women	65	6	29	= 100
Primary school	63	10	27	= 100
Secondary school	77	8	15	= 100
CDU/CSU supporters	94	×	6	= 100
SPD supporters	41	27	32	= 100
FDP/DVP supporters	82	7	11	= 100

Question put to persons who think Adenauer safeguards other interests:
"And what do you think is most important to him?"

August 1953

A	Total popu- lation %	Men %	Women %	Supporters: CDU/ CSU %	SPD %	FDP/ DVP %
The interests of the Catholic Church . . .	3	4	1	×	9	4
The interests of the Capitalists	2	3	1	×	7	×
The interests of foreign countries . . .	2	2	1	×	3	×
Personal, private interests	2	3	2	×	7	1
Other interests . . .	1	2	×	×	1	3
No statement	1	1	1	×	3	×
Remainder not questioned	90	86	94	100	73	93
Total	101	101	100	100	103	101

Question: "Do you believe that Adenauer makes equal efforts for all strata of the population, or that he gives preference to certain strata?"

September 1955

	The same for all	Favours certain strata	Un-decided	Total
	%	%	%	%
Total population	43	30	27	= 100
Men	42	36	22	= 100
Women	45	25	30	= 100
Agriculture	44	24	32	= 100
Workers.	36	35	29	= 100
Salaried employees, civil servants	51	27	22	= 100
Independent trades and professions	53	27	20	= 100
CDU/CSU supporters	72	12	16	= 100
SPD supporters	22	55	23	= 100
FDP/DVP supporters	47	33	20	= 100

Question put to people who believe that Adenauer favours certain strata:
"And what strata does he give preference to?"

September 1955

	Upper Class	Catho- lics	Party friends	Others	Unques- tioned re- mainder	Total
	%	%	%	%	%	%
Total population . .	17	8	2	7	70	= 104
Men	23	8	3	7	64	= 105
Women	12	7	2	7	75	= 103
Agriculture	14	6	1	7	76	= 104
Workers.	20	8	3	8	65	= 104
Salaried employees, civil servants	16	8	2	4	73	= 103
Independent trades and professions	15	9	2	5	73	= 104
CDU/CSU supporters	8	3	×	2	88	= 101
SPD supporters. . . .	34	11	5	11	45	= 106
FDP/DVP supporters .	16	17	2	5	67	= 107

Question: "It is said that Adenauer very actively supports the rearmament of West Germany. What do you think personally: Why does he do that?"

January 1952

	In the interests of Germany	In the interests of other countries	Out of egoism, in his own interests	Other answers	Don't know	Total
	%	%	%	%	%	%
Total population . . .	47	17	12	5	21	= 102
Men	51	20	15	5	12	= 103
Women	43	15	9	6	29	= 102
18—29 years old . .	45	16	15	4	23	= 103
30—44	45	19	12	6	19	= 101
45—59	48	17	11	5	21	= 102
60 and over	49	16	11	5	23	= 104
Primary school . . .	43	17	13	5	24	= 102
Secondary school . .	56	17	9	6	14	= 102
Secondary school graduates ("Abitur") .	66	19	8	3	7	= 103
North Germany . . .	48	17	12	4	23	= 104
West Germany. . . .	49	19	11	5	18	= 102
South Germany . . .	41	18	14	7	23	= 103
CDU/CSU supporters	73	10	3	2	14	= 102
SPD supporters. . . .	39	22	17	6	18	= 102
FDP/DVP supporters .	74	10	9	3	9	= 105
KPD supporters . . .	16	40	44	4	4	= 108
BP supporters	50	15	15	5	15	= 100
DP supporters	63	12	6	4	18	= 103
BHE supporters . . .	43	31	12	8	9	= 103
SRP supporters . . .	33	31	17	2	21	= 104

Question: "Apart from the generals, there is a statesman in every country who has supreme command over the army. Who ought that to be in our country: Adenauer, the Federal Chancellor, or Heuss, the President?"

January 1955

	%
Theodor Heuss	41
Konrad Adenauer	15
Neither	20
Undecided, don't know	24
Total	100

Question: "There is a lot of talk at present about whether Adenauer has done enough for reunification.

Some say: 'We could have made much more progress towards reunification, if Adenauer had accepted the Russian proposals in past years.'

Others say: 'Adenauer was unable to do any more for reunification, because the Russians have not made any acceptable proposals so far.'

Would you agree with the first group, or the second group?"

May 1959

A	Total popu-lation	Men	Women	Supporters: CDU/CSU	SPD	FDP/DVP
	%	%	%	%	%	%
The first ("We could have made more progress") . . .	28	36	22	12	52	30
The second ("Adenauer was unable to do any more") . .	44	46	43	69	27	55
Undecided	28	18	35	19	21	15
Total	100	100	100	100	100	100

Question: "Are you in favour of Adenauer's holding as strong a position as possible in the government, or should he not have so much freedom of action?"

August 1953

A	Should not have so much freedom of action	Favour strong position	Undecided	Total
	%	%	%	%
Total population	37	32	31	= 100
Men	49	36	15	= 100
Women	27	29	44	= 100
18—29 years old	37	26	37	= 100
30—44	43	28	29	= 100
45—59	34	37	29	= 100
60 and over	32	41	27	= 100
CDU/CSU supporters . .	12	66	22	= 100
SPD supporters.	75	10	15	= 100
FDP/DVP supporters . . .	23	55	22	= 100

Question: "It is often said of Adenauer that in recent years in West Germany he was so strong that he was able to have his own way. What is the position at present: Do you think Adenauer still has a firm hold of the reins in his party and the government, or no longer quite such a firm hold?"

	1956 July	1959 July
	%	%
No longer quite so firm	45	47
Firm	30	28
Undecided, no opinion	25	25
Total	100	100

APPROVAL, CRITICISM

III

Between 1949 and 1962, the Allensbach Institute put the question of whether the German public agreed with "Adenauer's policy" nearly 200 times. The results are shown in a diagram on the following pages. At the beginning of the graph, early in 1950, 28 per cent agreed with his policy; towards the end, in December 1961, it was fourty-three per cent.

The span between includes peaks and troughs. Experience in polls has shown that it is possible, in fortunate circumstances, to climb rapidly to a peak of popularity. But it is difficult to maintain a good average of general popularity over a protracted period. That seems to be a rarity in political life.

Fundamentally, there is no really specific criticism of his political actions. In 1956, one of the voters' main objections to Adenauer was that he was too old: but that did not prevent the majority from voting his party. And up to the present, the position has remained unchanged.

Question: "What do you think about Adenauer's policy so far?"

December 1949

	Total population	Men	Women	Supporters: CDU/ CSU	SPD	FDP/ DVP
	%	%	%	%	%	%
Excellent	3	4	2	7	×	5
Agree with it	20	20	19	40	8	31
Agree with certain reservations	23	31	18	22	31	32
Condemn it	15	19	11	3	30	4
No opinion	39	26	50	28	31	28
Total	100	100	100	100	100	100

Question: "Do you agree with Adenauer's policy on the whole?"

January 1950

	Agree	Dis-agree	Undecided, don't know	Total
	%	%	%	%
Total population	33	22	45	= 100
Men	38	28	34	= 100
Women	29	16	55	= 100
Under 30 years old	25	23	52	= 100
30—49	35	22	43	= 100
50—65	37	19	44	= 100
Over 65 years	35	17	48	= 100
Primary school	30	21	49	= 100
Secondary school	44	25	31	= 100
Secondary school graduates ("Abitur")	50	23	27	= 100
Workers.	27	27	46	= 100
Agricultural workers	23	22	55	= 100
Farmers	31	17	52	= 100
Salaried employees	41	18	41	= 100
Civil servants	52	13	35	= 100
Independent trades and crafts . .	39	13	48	= 100
Independent professions . . .	34	32	34	= 100
Pensioners	35	17	48	= 100
Unemployed	23	34	43	= 100
CDU/CSU supporters	59	7	34	= 100
SPD supporters	25	38	37	= 100
FDP/DVP supporters	57	12	31	= 100
KPD supporters	7	78	15	= 100
DRP supporters	37	33	30	= 100
BP supporters	35	16	49	= 100
Centre supportes	52	16	32	= 100
DP supporters	44	21	35	= 100

Question: "Do you agree or disagree with Adenauer's government on the whole?"

November 1951

A	Agree	Disagree	Undecided, don't know	Total
	%	%	%	%.
Total population	33	35	32	= 100
Men	37	45	18	= 100
Women	30	26	44	= 100
CDU/CSU supporters	62	11	27	= 100
SPD supporters	18	61	21	= 100
FDP/DVP supporters	55	31	14	= 100

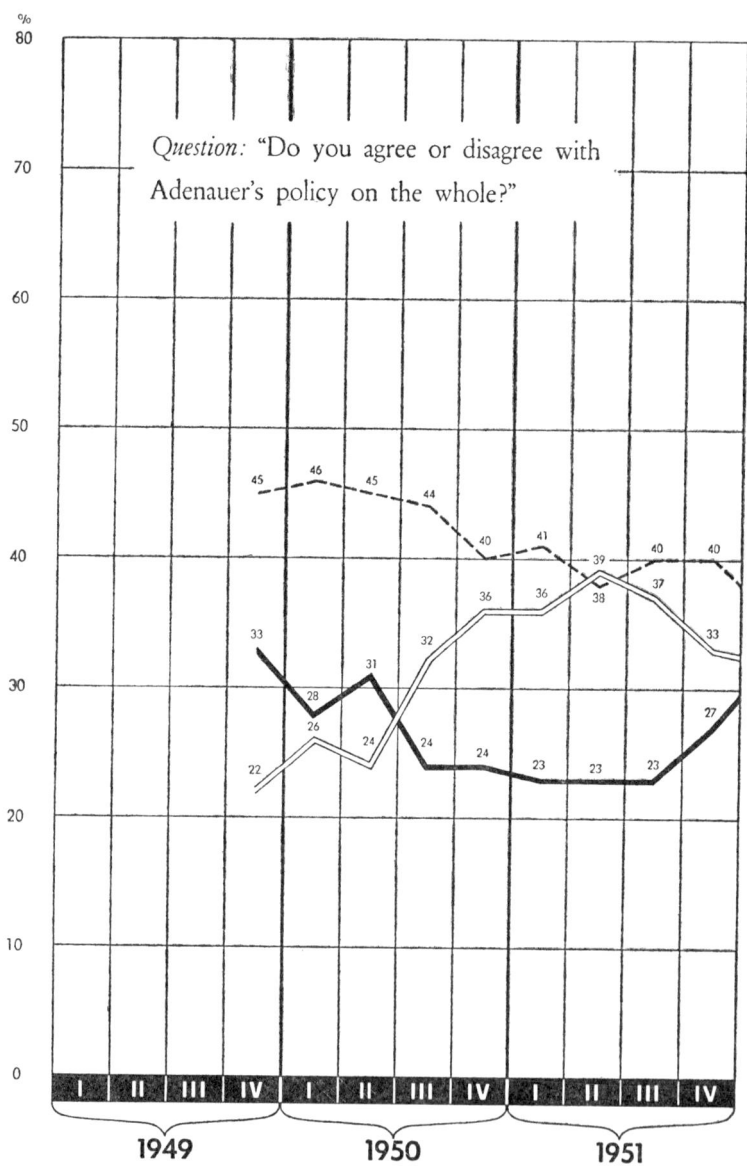

Question: "Do you agree or disagree with Adenauer's policy on the whole?"

45 46 45 44 40 41 39 40 40
36 36 38 37
33 32 33
31
28 27
26 24 24 24 23 23 23
22

| 1949 | 1950 | 1951 |
| I II III IV | I II III IV | I II III IV |

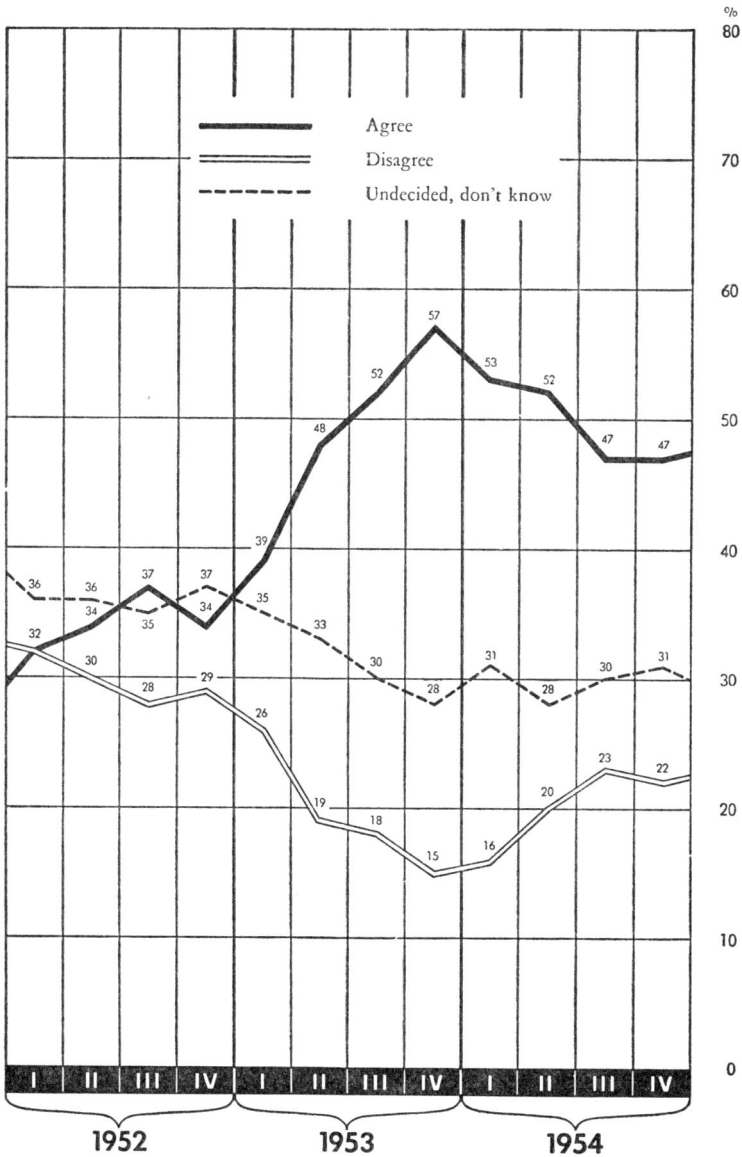

%
80

70

60

50

40

30

20

10

0

Agree
Disagree
Undecided, don't know

| I | II | III | IV | I | II | III | IV | I | II | III | IV |

1952   1953   1954

36 36 37 37 35
34   34 35 33
32   35   30
    30   29   26
      28
39 48 52 57 53 52 47 47

30 28 28 31 28 30 31
19 18 15 16 20 23 22

41

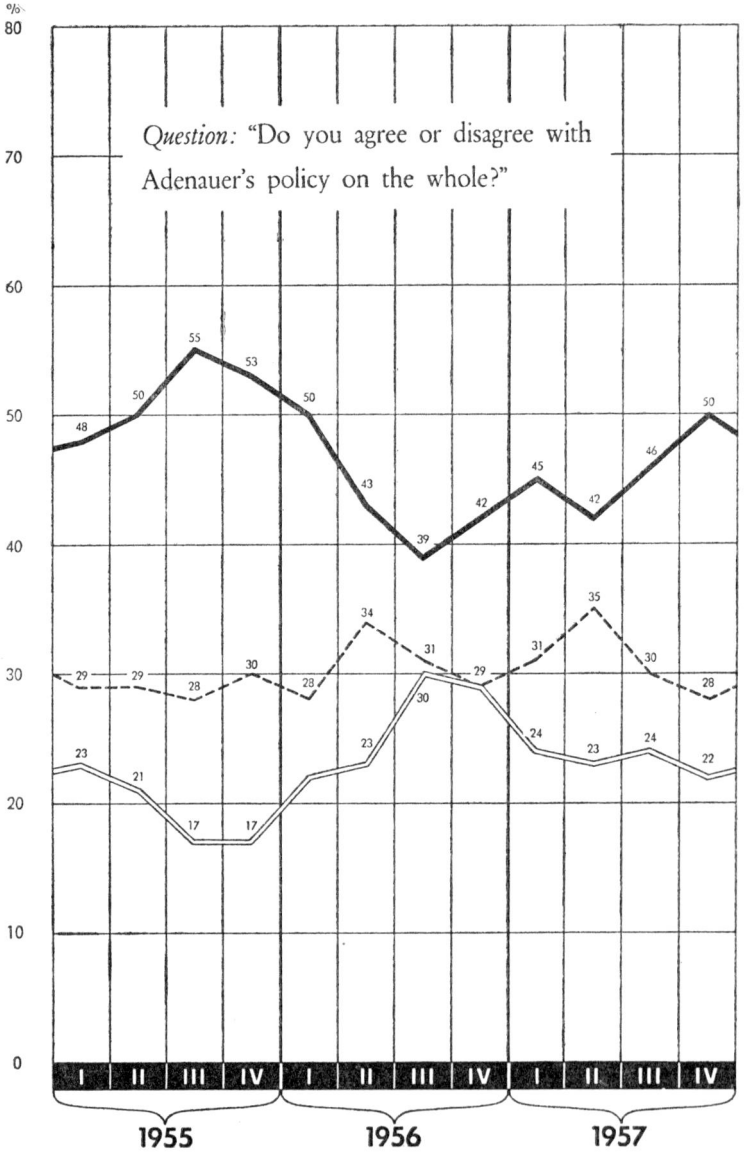

Question: "Do you agree or disagree with Adenauer's policy on the whole?"

1955   1956   1957

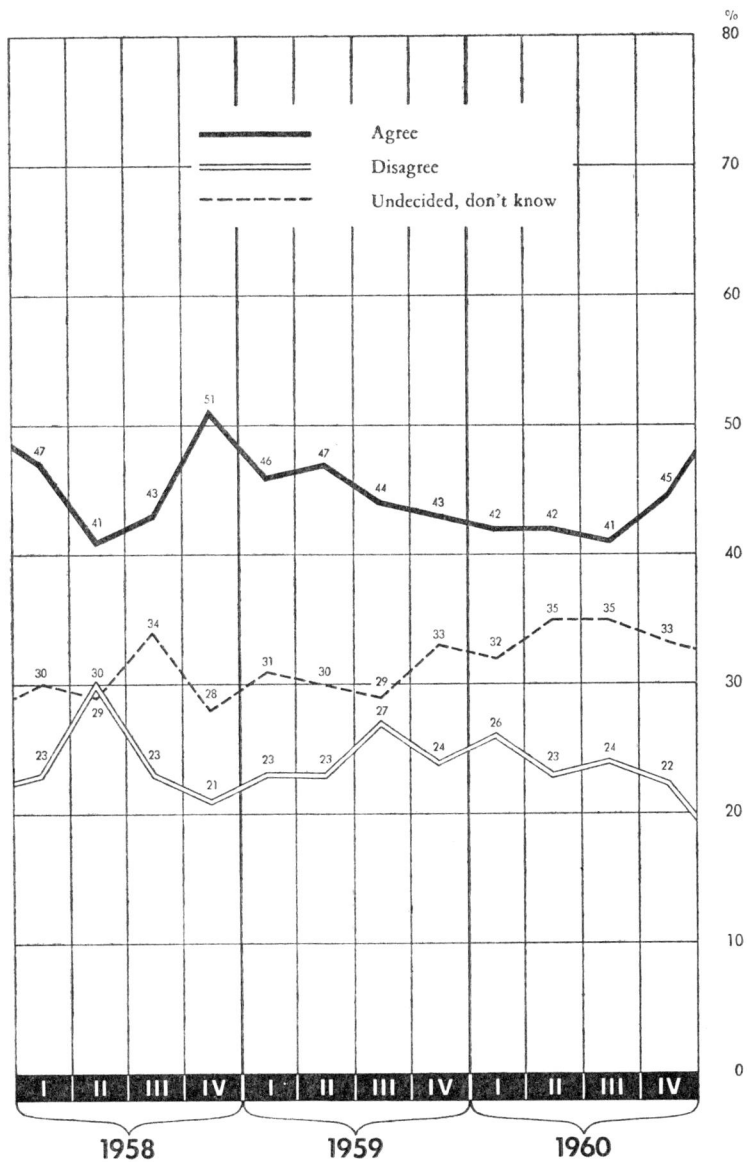

	Agree
	Disagree
	Undecided, don't know

47 41 43 51 46 47 44 43 42 42 41 45

34 30 30 31 30 29 33 32 35 35 33

30 29 28 23 23 27 26 23 24 22

23 29 23 21 23 23 24 24

I	II	III	IV	I	II	III	IV	I	II	III	IV
1958				1959				1960			

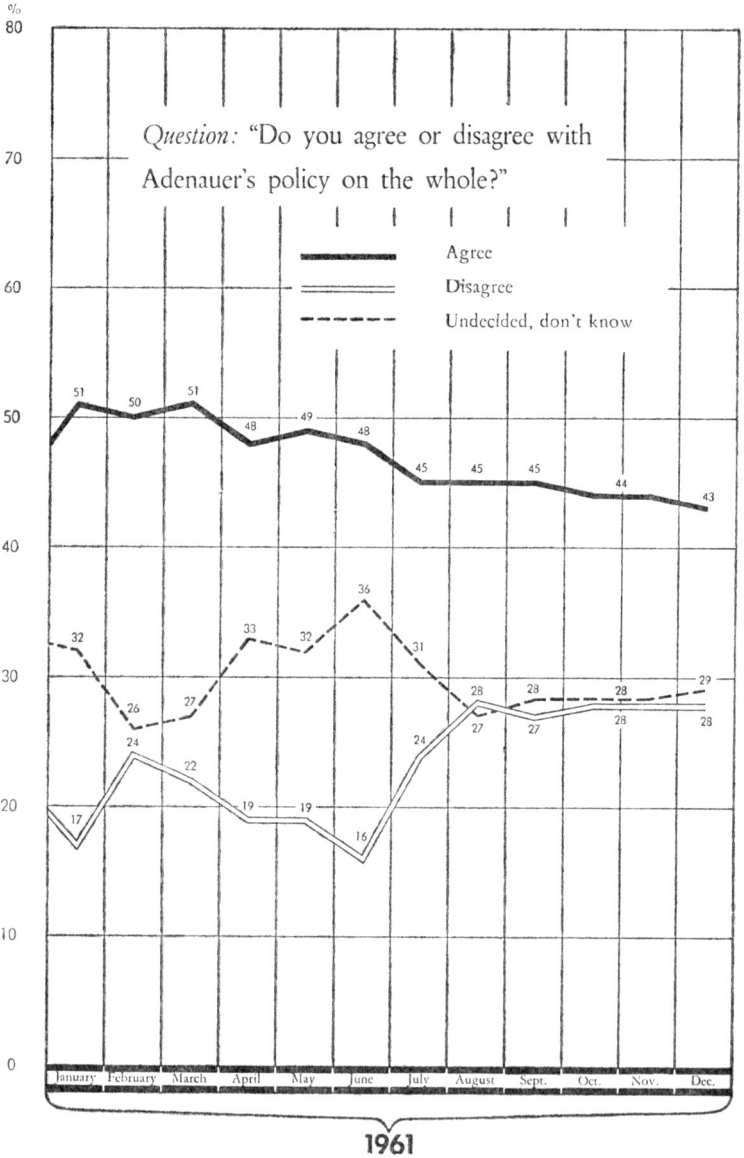

Question: "Do you agree or disagree with Adenauer's policy on the whole?"

Agree
Disagree
Undecided, don't know

1961

44

Question: "Would you please select the three points which you feel are most applicable to Adenauer?" (L)

	1953 February	1955 January
	%	%
"Adenauer is a good negotiator, has restored Germany's reputation"	55	70
"Adenauer wants to give us security against the East"	47	51
"Adenauer has ensured that we are better off economically"	45	55
"Adenauer rules tyrannically, will not recognize other opinions"	35	32
"Adenauer is not socially minded, does not do enough for the man in the street"	30	30
"Adenauer is driving us towards a war"	19	19
Don't know, none of these statements	18	11
Total	249	268

Question: "There are always some things in which people are dissatisfied with the government: Has Adenauer done or said anything in the past three months which you did not like?"

July 1953

	Total population	Men	Women	Supporters: CDU/CSU	SPD	FDP/DVP
	%	%	%	%	%	%
No	36	42	30	53	20	39
Yes	17	26	10	5	30	19
Don't know	47	32	60	42	50	42
Total	100	100	100	100	100	100

Question put to people who in the preliminary question said there was something about Adenauer's government they did not like in the past three months: "Could you tell me what it was you did not like?"

	Total popu- lation	Men	Women	Supporters: CDU/ CSU	SPD	FDP/ DVP
	%	%	%	%	%	%
Obstinate attitude to- wards the East, neglect of reunification . . .	4	5	3	1	6	4
The European Defence agreement, attitude to rearmament	4	7	2	2	8	5
Neglect of social mat- ters	3	4	2	1	6	1
Dependence on the western powers, neglect of German interests	2	3	1	×	3	2
Attitude on the Saar question	1	1	×	×	1	1
Too authoritarian. . .	1	2	×	×	1	2
Too much dominated by Church and deno- minational considera- tions	1	1	×	×	1	×
Restitution to Israel . .	×	×	×	×	×	×
Other things	4	6	2	1	8	6
No (definite) statement	1	1	1	×	1	1
Remainder not questioned	83	74	90	95	70	81
Total	104	104	101	100	105	103

Question put to people who in a preliminary question said there was something about Adenauer's government they did not like in the past three months: "Could you tell me what it was you did not like?"

January 1954

	Total popu- lation %	Men %	Women %	Supporters: CDU/ CSU %	SPD %	FDP/ DVP %
Neglect of social matters	6	7	5	3	12	5
The European Defence agreement, attitude to rearmament	5	6	3	1	12	4
Obstinate attitude towards the East, neglect of reunification . . .	3	5	2	1	9	5
Creation of new Federal ministries	1	1	1	×	1	3
Too much dominated by Church and denominational considerations	1	2	1	1	1	4
Other things	7	11	4	4	11	9
No (definite) statement	×	×	×	1	1	×
Remainder not questioned.	80	71	87	91	60	75
Total	103	103	103	102	107	105

Question: "Two men are discussing the present situation. One says: 'Adenauer has had a number of successes. But now his policy has finally failed and his period of greatness is past.' The other says: 'Despite all the current difficulties, Adenauer will find a way and in the end manage everything for the best.' Which of them do you agree with?"

October 1954

	%
"Adenauer will manage everything for the best"	58
"Adenauer's period of greatness is past"	13
Undecided, don't know	29
Total	100

Question: "A great variety of objections are made about Adenauer; here is a series of them. Could you tell me what objection (chief objection) you have regarding him?" (L) (^{1})

	1951 June	1956 February	1959 May
	%	%	%
Too compliant towards the West	19	20	12
Does too little for reunification	—	20	21
Not socially minded	15	25	19
Too old	12	27	44
Too dependent on the Church	11	24	24
His attitude to rearmament.	7	21	—
His attitude to nuclear armament	—	—	22
Too dictatorial	3	17	—
Obstinate, not flexible enough	—	—	21
Too inflexible in his attitude towards Russia	—	—	21
Always sticks to the same policy, has no new ideas	—	—	23
Other objections	1	2	1
No objections to Adenauer.	16	26	21
Don't know	16	12	12
Total	100	194	241

Question: "Could you tell me what you don't like (about Adenauer's policy), what you don't agree with?"

	1955 March	1956 September	1957 May

A

	%	%	%
Rearmament	14	18	17
Economic and social policy	10	15	12
The Saar agreement	7	—	—
The Paris Agreements	1	—	—
Foreign policy, dependence on the Western powers	5	9	4
Neglect of reunification	3	6	4
Too dictatorial	3	4	2
Too dominated by denominational considerations	2	3	1
Adenauer is too old	—	2	1
Other reasons	5	6	6
No (definite) statement	3	4	4
Remainder not questioned	56	46	57
Total	109	113	108

Question: "Could you tell me what you like (about Adenauer's policy), what you agree with?"

	1956 July	1960 August

A

	%	%
His successes are undeniable	18	15
The "economic miracle"	—	13
He is a great statesman	5	—
His European policy, his foreign policy	3	5
His being a professed Christian	1	—
Other favourable statements	14	5
Don't know, no (definite) statement	5	5
Remainder not questioned	55	59
Total	101	102

Question: "Would you please choose five cards with the statements you feel are most applicable to Adenauer?" (K)

October 1956

	Total popu-lation %	Men %	Wo-men %	18-29 %	30-44 %	45-59 %	60 and over %
					Age groups:		
"Adenauer knows best how to deal with foreign countries" .	52	50	55	48	52	53	56
"Adenauer wants to give us security against the East and ensures that we are protected by the Western defence pact"	40	43	37	39	38	42	43
"Adenauer is still the best man we have"	37	36	37	33	34	38	43
"What I like about Adenauer is that he favours Christian principles in politics" . . .	34	30	38	27	33	36	44
"Adenauer ensures prosperity and that everybody has work"	31	31	32	32	28	33	33
"Adenauer does too little to keep prices stable"	59	61	58	59	63	59	55
"Adenauer does too little for reunification of Germany, ne-gotiates too little with the Russians"	51	56	46	52	55	50	45
"Adenauer is too old" . . .	48	51	44	50	50	48	42
"Adenauer's defence policy is injurious"	41	45	38	47	43	41	31
"Adenauer lets himself be in-fluenced by the Church too much"	41	48	36	41	45	43	35
No comment	4	3	5	5	4	2	6
Total	438	454	426	433	445	445	433

Question: "Here are a few sentences that are sometimes heard in conversation. Would you pick out for me all the sentences which you think are correct?"

February 1957

A	Total population	Men	Women
	%	%	%
"Adenauer has put Germany on its feet again, and gained respect for us in the world"	59	60	59
"What I like about Adenauer is that he favours Christian principles in politics"	36	36	36
"Adenauer ensures prosperity and that everybody has work"	35	39	32
"I appreciate it that Adenauer does so much for pensioners"	25	23	26
"I think it is right for Adenauer to make such great efforts to build up an army"	24	28	20
"I like the fact that Adenauer does so much for German reunification"	23	23	24
"Adenauer does too little to keep prices stable"	47	49	45
"Adenauer does too little for reunification of Germany"	39	45	32
"Adenauer favours the military much too much" .	31	32	30
"Adenauer lets himself be influenced by the Church too much"	30	37	23
"Adenauer does much too little for the simple worker"	30	35	26
"What I don't like about Adenauer is that he does too little for pensioners"	25	28	23
None of them	5	3	6
Total	409	438	382

54

Question: "Four men are talking about Adenauer. Which of their opinions comes closest to what you think?" (B)

February 1957

	Total popu- lation %	Men %	Women %	Supporters: CDU/ CSU %	SPD %
The first says: "Adenauer should remain Federal Chancellor. What comes afterwards is seldom any better"	27	26	28	29	17
The second says: "Adenauer should remain Federal Chancellor whatever happens. He is the most capable man we have"	24	23	24	51	×
The third says: "We ought to try somebody else. The time will come when somebody else will have to do the job"	23	24	22	12	30
The fourth says: "We absolutely must have a new Federal Chancellor. There are younger men who are capable of more than Adenauer"	17	23	13	4	45
No comment	9	4	13	4	8
Total	100	100	100	100	100

Question: "Would you please choose five cards with statements you feel are most applicable to Adenauer?" (K)

February 1958

A	Total population	Men	Women
	%	%	%
"Adenauer knows best how to deal with foreign countries"	56	51	60
"Adenauer wants to give us security against the East and ensures that we are protected by the Western defence pact"	46	43	48
"Adenauer is still the best man we have" .	45	41	48
"Adenauer ensures prosperity and that everybody has work"	36	32	39
"What I like about Adenauer is thathe favours Christian principles in politics". .	33	27	39
"Adenauer does too little to keep prices stable"	61	67	56
"Adenauer does too little for reunification of Germany"	45	53	38
"Adenauer is too old"	44	50	38
"Adenauer lets himself be influenced by the Church too much"	39	48	31
"Adenauer's defence policy is injurious" . .	32	39	26
No comment	4	2	5
Total	441	453	428

Question: "When you think about the time since the last elections, do you find that Adenauer took advantage of the CDU majority in the Bundestag to keep, by and large, the promises he made before the elections, or has Adenauer failed to keep his promises?"

September 1959

A	Total popu- lation	Men	Women	Supporters: CDU/ CSU	SPD	FDP/ DVP
	%	%	%	%	%	%
Adenauer's promises have been:						
Kept, by and large . .	36	37	33	63	18	31
Not kept	30	40	23	9	59	45
Undecided	14	14	15	13	13	10
Don't know	20	9	29	15	10	14
Total	100	100	100	100	100	100

Question: "Do you think that, on the whole, Adenauer has acted correctly or incorrectly in the latest Berlin crisis?"

August 1961

	Correctly %	Incorrectly %	Undecided %	Total %
Total population	32	41	27	= 100
Men	31	49	20	= 100
Women	33	34	33	= 100
Electors in German Federal Republic *excluding* West Berlin:				
CDU/CSU supporters	61	15	24	= 100
SPD supporters	11	69	20	= 100
FDP supporters	26	48	26	= 100

RIVALS AND SUCCESSORS

IV

Now, as this book is going into print, Adenauer has been Chancellor of the Federal Republic of Germany for 13 years without interruption. When he was elected to that office for the first time in 1949, it depended on a single vote whether he would make it or not. He got in, with the help of his own vote.

No wonder, then, that many rivals reckoned on a chance for themselves. They speculated on the one hand on the head of government not being able to hold out for long with such a limited parliamentary support, and, on the other hand, on the natural necessity for a successor in 1953. But things turned out differently. Many of his strongest political opponents left the arena before him or gave up the struggle. All forecasts of his leaving the political stage were wrong, as have been all nominations of successors so far. So we prefer to refrain from making any.

Question: "Do you think it would be better if some one other than Adenauer became head of the Government?"

	1951 January	June
	%	%
Yes, would be better	26	35
No, would not be better	33	33
Undecided, indifferent	41	32
Total	100	100

Question: "Assuming that in the next elections it were not possible to vote for parties, but only for individuals: Here is a list with twelve names. Who would you most like to see at the head of the government?" (L)

September 1952

	Total popu- lation %	Men %	Women %	Supporters: CDU/ CSU %	SPD %	FDP/ DVP %
Konrad Adenauer . .	24	23	26	60	8	26
Theodor Heuss . . .	17	13	20	21	12	27
Erich Ollenhauer . .	10	13	7	1	37	1
Carlo Schmid	5	7	3	1	15	2
Ernst Reuter	4	5	4	2	9	3
Ernst Remer . . .	3	4	1	1	1	1
Hermann Ehlers . . .	3	4	2	2	2	8
Franz Blücher	3	4	2	×	2	17
Karl Arnold	2	3	1	2	2	2
Helene Wessel	2	1	2	1	1	1
Waldemar Kraft . . .	2	3	1	×	1	×
H.-Ch. Seebohm . .	1	2	1	×	×	1
None of them . . .	7	8	6	2	2	4
Doesn't matter. . . .	16	8	23	7	8	6
No answer	1	2	1	×	×	1
Total	100	100	100	100	100	100

Question: "In the autumn the new Bundestag will be elected. Would you consider it a good thing for Adenauer to remain Federal Chancellor for another four years, or do you think it would be better for some other man to become head of the government?"

April 1953

	Adenauer should remain	Different Federal Chancellor better	Don't know	Total
	%	%	%	%
Total population	48	25	27	= 100
Men	49	32	19	= 100
Women	48	19	33	= 100
18—29 years old	47	25	28	= 100
30—44	45	31	24	= 100
45—49	48	25	27	= 100
60 and over	55	18	27	= 100
CDU/CSU supporters	85	5	10	= 100
SPD supporters	24	58	18	= 100
FDP/DVP supporters	69	18	13	= 100

Question put to persons who think it would be better for some person other than Adenauer to become head of the government: "Who, in your opinion, ought to become Federal Chancellor?"

April 1953

	Total popu- laton	Men	Women	Supporters: CDU/ CSU	SPD	FDP/ DVP
	%	%	%	%	%	%
Erich Ollenhauer . .	5	8	3	×	21	1
Carlo Schmid	1	2	×	×	5	1
Ernst Reuter	1	1	×	×	2	×
Other politicians . . .	3	4	2	1	2	7
No names given . .	15	17	14	4	28	9
Remainder not questioned	75	68	81	95	42	82
Total	100	100	100	100	100	100

Question: "In the autumn the Bundestag must elect a new Federal Chancellor. Here is a list: Which of these three men would be best as Federal Chancellor?" (L)

(Baden-Württemberg)   *June 1953*

	Total popu- lation	Men	Women	Supporters: CDU/ CSU	SPD	FDP/ DVP
	%	%	%	%	%	%
Konrad Adenauer . .	45	46	44	83	24	51
Erich Ollenhauer . .	15	19	11	1	43	6
Reinhold Maier . . .	11	13	10	4	14	26
Neither of them . . .	9	10	9	4	7	9
Undecided, don't know	20	12	26	8	12	8
Total	100	100	100	100	100	100

Question: "Do you think it would be better if someone other than Adenauer became head of the Government?"

	1955 February	1956 February	1956 June
	%	%	%
Yes, would be better	20	20	30
No, would not be better	55	53	45
Undecided, indifferent	25	27	25
Total	100	100	100

Question put to persons who think it would be better for some man other than Adenauer to become head of the government: "Who do you have in mind?"

	1955 February	1956 February
	%	%
Erich Ollenhauer	5	6
Other SPD politicians	4	2
Heinrich von Brentano	×	×
Other CDU politicians	1	1
FDP politicians	1	1
Other names	1	×
No definite suggestion	9	11
Total	21	21

Question: "Let us assume that Adenauer resigns from office: Do you think that the outcome would be favourable or unfavourable for us?"

November 1955

	Unfavour-able	Favour-able	Don't know	Total
	%	%	%	%
Total population	43	9	48	= 100
Men	45	12	43	= 100
Women	41	7	52	= 100
CDU/CSU supporters	64	5	31	= 100
SPD supporters	23	22	55	= 100
FDP/DVP supporters	52	13	35	= 100

Question put to persons who think the outcome would be unfavourable if Adenauer resigned from office: "Do you think it would be a very heavy blow for us, or would it soon be overcome?"

November 1955

	%
Would be a heavy blow	26
Would soon be overcome	13
Don't know	4
Remainder not questioned	57
Total	100

Question: "Assuming that Adenauer plans to resign tomorrow: Which of these men would you prefer to see as his successor?" (L)

November 1955

	Total popu- lation %	Men %	Women %	Supporters: CDU/ CSU %	SPD %	FDP/ DVP %
Heinrich von Brentano	20	23	17	29	17	16
Franz Blücher	9	10	7	8	10	21
Karl Arnold	6	10	3	7	9	8
Ludwig Erhard . . .	5	6	5	6	4	9
Eugen Gerstenmaier .	5	6	5	7	6	2
Fritz Schäffer	4	5	2	6	2	6
None of them . . .	13	20	8	6	28	11
Don't know, no answer	38	20	53	31	24	27
Total	100	100	100	100	100	100

Question: "Do you think it would be better to have a younger man at the head of the government?"

August 1956

	Yes	No	Doesn't matter	Don't know	Total
	%	%	%	%	%
Total population	45	31	24	×	= 100
Men	52	32	16	×	= 100
Women	38	30	31	1	= 100
18—29 years old	43	29	28	×	= 100
30—44	48	30	22	×	= 100
45—59	47	30	22	1	= 100
60 and over	38	35	26	1	= 100
CDU/CSU supporters	25	58	16	1	= 100
SPD supporters	70	14	15	1	= 100
FDP/DVP supporters	59	26	14	1	= 100

Question: "In the autumn of 1957 the new Bundestag will be elected. Would you consider it a good thing for Adenauer to remain Federal Chancellor for another four years, or do you think it would be better for some other man to become head of the government?"

July 1956

	Different Federal Chancellor better	Adenauer should remain	Don't know	Total
	%	%	%	%
Total population	43	35	22	= 100
Men	54	31	15	= 100
Women	33	39	28	= 100
CDU/CSU supporters	20	69	11	= 100
SPD supporters	75	13	12	= 100
FDP/DVP supporters	59	28	13	= 100

Question put to persons who think it would be better for some person other than Adenauer to become head of the government at the coming Bundestag elections in autumn 1957: "Who, in your opinion, ought to become Federal Chancellor?"

July 1956

	Total popu-lation	Men	Women	Supporters: CDU/ CSU	SPD	FDP/ DVP
	%	%	%	%	%	%
Erich Ollenhauer . .	6	11	3	×	23	5
Heinrich von Brentano	3	4	2	6	2	2
Thomas Dehler . . .	1	2	×	×	1	10
Other names	6	9	3	2	13	9
No statement	28	31	26	13	39	39
Remainder not questioned	57	46	67	80	25	41
Total	101	103	101	101	103	106

Question: "Would you say that you (personally) would have got on better in the last few years, if we had had an SPD government and not Adenauer at the helm?"

July 1955

	No	Yes	Undecided, don't know	Total
	%	%	%	%
Total population	38	11	51	= 100
Men	43	16	41	= 100
Women	34	7	59	= 100
CDU/CSU supporters	68	×	32	= 100
SPD supporters	14	40	46	= 100
FDP/DVP supporters	71	4	25	= 100

Question: "Who would you rather see as Federal Chancellor: Someone from the SPD or Adenauer?"

February 1957

	Adenauer	Someone from the SPD	Undecided	Other answers	Total
	%	%	%	%	%
Total population .	46	24	27	3	= 100
Men	46	30	21	3	= 100
Women	46	18	33	3	= 100
CDU/CSU supporters	88	2	7	3	= 100
SPD supporters . .	10	70	19	1	= 100

Question: "And if Adenauer were no longer Federal Chancellor now would you rather have a Chancellor from the CDU/CSU or one from the SPD?"

February 1957

	From the CDU/CSU	From the SPD	Undecided	Other answers	Total
	%	%	%	%	%
Total population .	37	31	31	1	= 100
Men	34	37	26	3	= 100
Women	40	25	35	×	= 100
CDU/CSU supporters	80	3	15	2	= 100
SPD supporters . .	4	81	14	1	= 100

Question: "And who would you favour as the new Federal Chancellor?"

February 1957

	%
Heinrich von Brentano	12
Erich Ollenhauer	11
Carlo Schmid	4
Karl Arnold	3
Kurt Georg Kiesinger	1
Franz-Josef Strauß	1
Thomas Dehler	1
Other CDU politicians	7
Other SPD politicians	4
Undecided	26
No (definite) statement	32
Total	102

Question: "You can never really know what things will be like in the future. But if Adenauer remains Federal Chancellor, what do you think the political situation will be like in the next three or four years? Could you choose a statement from this list to express your opinion?" (L)

February 1957

	Total popu- lation	Men	Women	Supporters: CDU/ CSU	SPD
	%	%	%	%	%
"Adenauer's greatest period is over, but he will also achieve many great things in the future"	33	34	33	38	20
"If Adenauer remains, he will have many great successes as he has now"	26	28	25	50	10
"If Adenauer remains, he will let many things take their course, and our political position will slowly decline"	12	15	10	1	25
"Adenauer will get snarled up, and there are bound to be serious setbacks"	11	13	9	×	24
"If Adenauer continues as Federal Chancellor, he will show his real greatness in the next few years"	7	9	6	14	5
"If Adenauer continues as Federal Chancellor, it may prove a great misfortune for us" . . .	5	8	2	1	14
None of these statements . . .	13	8	18	5	16
Total	107	115	103	109	114

Question: "Assuming that a new decision had to be made on who is to be Federal Chancellor and there were only two possibilities: Adenauer or Erhard, who would you prefer as Federal Chancellor?"

	1960 December	1961 April	1961 July
	%	%	%
Adenauer	31	31	33
Erhard	33	34	33
Undecided, don't care	36	35	34
Total	100	100	100

Question: "Assuming that a new decision had to be made on who is to be Federal Chancellor and there were only two possibilities: Adenauer or Willy Brandt, who would you prefer as Federal Chancellor?"

	1960 December	1961 February	1961 April	1961 June	1961 August	1961 September
	%	%	%	%	%	%
Adenauer	34	38	35	41	34	35
Willy Brandt . . .	34	34	33	28	36	30
Undecided, don't care	32	28	32	31	30	35
Total	100	100	100	100	100	100

Question: "Do you happen to know how long Adenauer said he would remain in office — does he intend to remain Federal Chancellor for the next four years, or does he intend to hand his office over to his successor earlier?"

December 1961

	Hand over office earlier	Remain Federal Chancellor for another 4 years	Don't know	Total
	%	%	%	%
Total population	68	11	21	= 100
Men	78	10	12	= 100
Women.	60	12	28	= 100
CDU/CSU supporters . .	69	12	19	= 100
SPD supporters	70	12	18	= 100
FDP/DVP supporters . . .	80	8	12	= 100

Question put to persons who knew that Adenauer said he would relinquish his office before the end of the legislative period: "What do you think — is it probable that Adenauer will relinquish his office or retain it?"

December 1961

	Relinquish	Retain	Impossible to say	Remainder not questioned	Total
	%	%	%	%	%
Total population	31	23	14	32	= 100
Men	38	27	13	22	= 100
Women.	27	19	14	40	= 100
CDU/CSU supporters . .	41	16	12	31	= 100
SPD supporters	25	31	14	30	= 100
FDP/DVP supporters . . .	42	26	12	20	= 100

PRESIDENT OR CHANCELLOR?

V

There is one weak spot in the astounding career of Chancellor Adenauer. Once he hesitatingly agreed to resign from office to let himself be nominated for the Federal Presidency. At that time — in 1959 — this decision was welcomed not only by many politicians, but also by a large proportion of the population. With a cunning that the public instinct sometimes reveals, it was believed possible in this way to get rid of him and yet still keep him. For people wanted to get rid of him, because they thought a younger man was needed; but they also wanted to keep him, because they felt dependent on his personality and his experience, and will continue to do so as long as he heads the government.

It was a long time before the public forgave him for changing his hesitant decision. But they did forgive him.

Question: "Next year the members of the Bundestag have to elect a
new Federal President. What do you think: Who, in your opinion
should become Federal President, who would you nominate?"

December 1953

A	Total popu-lation	Men	Women	Supporters: CDU/ CSU	SPD	FDP/ DVP
	%	%	%	%	%	%
Theodor Heuss . . .	42	44	40	53	38	62
Konrad Adenauer . .	2	3	2	5	1	1
Erich Ollenhauer . .	2	2	1	×	7	×
Hermann Ehlers . . .	1	2	×	1	×	3
Another man	3	4	2	2	3	4
No specific name . . .	3	4	2	3	4	5
Don't know	47	41	53	36	47	25
Total	100	100	100	100	100	100

Question: "Have you heard that Adenauer intends to let himself be nominated for the Federal Presidency, or is this the first you have heard of it?"

	1959 April	May
	%	%
Yes, heard about it	91	94
First I've heard of it	9	6
Total	100	100

Question: "Do you welcome or regret it that Adenauer plans to relinquish his office as Federal Chancellor and become Federal President?"

April 1959

A	Welcome it	Regret it	Undecided	Total
	%	%	%	%
Total population	36	18	46	= 100
Men	39	20	41	= 100
Women	33	17	50	= 100
CDU/CSU supporters	41	23	36	= 100
SPD supporters	37	18	45	= 100
FDP/DVP supporters	54	19	27	= 100

Question put to persons who *welcome* it that Adenauer plans to relinquish his office as Federal Chancellor and become Federal President: "Could you explain that a little more precisely?"

April 1959

A	Satis-faction that Adenauer is resigning as *Chancellor*	Satis-faction that Adenauer will become *Federal President*	No (definite) answer	Remainder not questioned	Total
	%	%	%	%	%
Total population . .	21	12	3	64	= 100
Men	26	11	2	61	= 100
Women	17	13	3	67	= 100
CDU/CSU supporters	15	23	3	59	= 100
SPD supporters . . .	30	4	3	63	= 100
FDP/DVP supporters	42	12	×	46	= 100

Question put to persons who *regret* that Adenauer plans to relinquish his office as Federal Chancellor and become Federal President: "Could you explain that a little more precisely?"

April 1959

A	Regret that Adenauer is resigning as *Chancellor*	Regret that Adenauer will become *Federal President*	No (definite) answer	Remainder not questioned	Total
	%	%	%	%	%
Total population . . .	11	6	1	82	= 100
Men	11	7	2	80	= 100
Women	11	5	1	83	= 100
CDU/CSU supporters .	19	2	2	77	= 100
SPD supporters	6	11	1	82	= 100
FDP/DVP supporters .	11	8	×	81	= 100

Question: "What do you, personally, think would be better for Germany: for Adenauer to remain Federal Chancellor, or for him to become Federal President?"

April 1959

	Become Federal President	Stay Federal Chancellor	Other answers	Undecided	Total
	%	%	%	%	%
Total population . .	32	25	12	31	= 100
Men	38	25	15	22	= 100
Women	26	25	9	40	= 100
CDU/CSU supporters	39	33	2	26	= 100
SPD supporters . .	35	18	22	25	= 100

Question: "Suppose that two men are talking about what it would mean if Adenauer became Federal President.
The first says: 'Adenauer wants to get rid of the detail work. When he is President, he can give more attention to general political policy. Of course, he will continue to be responsible for the policy of the Federal Government.'
The second says: 'I don't think that that is the position at all. As President, Adenauer won't be concerned with high-level politics. Other people will have the responsibility — and there may be a lot of changes.'
Which of the two expresses what you think about it?" (B)

April 1959

A	Total population	Men	Women
	%	%	%
The second (Others responsible — may be a lot of changes)	42	48	38
The first (As President, continued responsibility for policies)	33	34	31
Undecided	25	18	31
Total	100	100	100

Question: "What is your personal opinion: Is it good or bad for Germany that Adenauer will be giving up his office of Federal Chancellor in a few months?"

April 1959

A	Good %	Bad %	Undecided %	Total %
Total population . .	38	19	43	= 100
Men	49	19	32	= 100
Women	30	19	51	= 100
CDU/CSU supporters	32	32	36	= 100
SPD supporters . . .	56	14	30	= 100
FDP/DVP supporters .	56	21	23	= 100

Question put to persons who think it bad for Germany for Adenauer to relinquish his office as Federal Chancellor: "Could you explain that more precisely?"

April 1959

A	Regret that he is relinquishing office of Chancellor	Regret that he will become President	No (definite) answer	Remainder not questioned	Total
	%	%	%	%	%
Total population . .	14	2	3	81	= 100
Men	14	2	3	81	= 100
Women	15	2	2	81	= 100
CDU/CSU supporters	27	1	4	68	= 100
SPD supporters . . .	8	4	2	86	= 100
FDP/DVP supporters .	15	3	3	79	= 100

Question: "Did you happen to hear on the radio or television the speech in which Adenauer explained why he is letting himself be nominated as Federal President?"

April 1959

	Heard all of it	Heard part of it	No	Total
	%	%	%	%
Total population . .	22	14	64	= 100
Men	30	10	60	= 100
Women	16	16	68	= 100

Question: "Why do you think Adenauer wants to give up his office as Federal Chancellor and have himself nominated for the Federal Presidency — which of the items in this list, do you think, are contributory reasons?" (L)

April 1959

A	%
"So that the CDU can find Adenauer's successor while the latter is still alive, and he himself can show his successor the ropes"	37
"For health reasons, he wants to save his strength"	35
"Because he is the only man in the CDU who can stand up against Carlo Schmid"	33
"Because Adenauer sees that his policies have failed and he wants to avoid having to accept the responsibility"	20
"Because the Americans want to pursue a new policy of understanding towards the Russians, and Adenauer does not agree with it"	16
"Because the CDU asked him to do so and he did not want to say 'no' "	14
"Because of the difficulties with the British, because the British have attacked his policies"	13
"Because the Russians exerted such great pressure that Adenauer felt he could make no headway against it"	12
"Because he has lost respect in his own party, no longer has the full confidence of the CDU"	11
Other answers	1
Don't know	12
Total	204

Question: "As things look at the moment, Adenauer and Carlo Schmid will be nominated for the office of Federal President. If you had your way, who would become President: Adenauer or Carlo Schmid?"

April 1959

A	Adenauer	Carlo Schmid	Undecided, don't care	Other answers	Total
	%	%	%	%	%
Total population . .	39	32	27	2	= 100
Men	38	42	17	3	= 100
Women	38	24	37	1	= 100
CDU/CSU supporters	76	8	16	×	= 100
SPD supporters . . .	10	68	20	2	= 100
FDP/DVP supporters .	42	42	12	4	= 100

Question: "If Adenauer gives up his office as Federal Chancellor and becomes Federal President — what do you think will happen: Will German foreign policy change or not?"

April 1959

	No change	Change: Quite a lot	Only a little	Undecided	Total
	%	%	%	%	%
Total population . .	47	11	16	26	= 100
Men	52	14	18	16	= 100
Women	43	7	14	36	= 100
CDU/CSU supporters	56	9	13	22	= 100
SPD supporters . . .	41	20	19	20	= 100

Question: "If Adenauer gives up his office, another man from the CDU must become Federal Chancellor. Which of the men listed here would you prefer as Federal Chancellor?" (L)

	1959 *April*	*May*
	%	%
Ludwig Erhard	38	42
Eugen Gerstenmaier	15	11
Heinrich von Brentano	6	5
Franz Etzel	4	5
Fritz Schäffer	2	1
Franz-Josef Strauß	1	2
Gerhard Schröder	1	1
Undecided, don't know	33	33
Total	100	100

Question: "Do you think that Adenauer's decision is final or not?"

1959
April   June

	%	%
Final	63	44
Not yet final	9	20
Impossible to say	19	27
Heard nothing about Adenauer's decision	9	9
Total	100	100

96

Question: "Have you heard that Adenauer no longer intends to become Federal President, but now wants to remain Federal Chancellor?"

	1959 June	July
	%	%
Heard about it	91	93
Heard nothing about it	9	7
Total	100	100

Question put to persons who have heard that Adenauer no longer intends to become Federal President, but now wants to remain Federal Chancellor: "Do you think that, all in all, it was a good or bad decision for Adenauer to want to remain Federal Chancellor?"

June 1959

	Bad decision	Good decision	Undecided	Remainder not questioned	Total
	%	%	%	%	%
Total population . .	43	23	25	9	= 100
Men	53	25	17	5	= 100
Women	21	34	32	13	= 100
CDU/CSU supporters	24	45	25	6	= 100
SPD supporters . . .	67	9	15	9	= 100

Question: "Did you happen to hear on the radio or television the speech in which Adenauer explained why he plans to remain Federal Chancellor?"

June 1959

	Heard all of it	Heard part of it	No	Heard nothing of Adenauer's decision	Total
	%	%	%	%	%
Total population . .	13	11	67	9	= 100
Men	17	11	67	5	= 100
Women	10	10	67	13	= 100
CDU/CSU supporters	16	12	66	6	= 100
SPD supporters . . .	15	11	65	9	= 100

Question put to persons who have heard that Adenauer no longer intends to become Federal President, but now prefers to remain Federal Chancellor: "Why do you think Adenauer wants to keep his office as Federal Chancellor? In your opinion, which of the items in this list are contributory reasons?" (L)

June 1959

A	Total popu- lation %	Men %	Women %
Because Adenauer is too fond of power and is just incapable of relinquishing power at the right time	39	49	30
Because he has realized that as Federal President he would no longer have enough influence on policy.	34	45	25
Because, in the meantime, foreign relations have become so difficult that Adenauer does not want to relinquish the helm	25	20	30
Because Adenauer is too old and no longer really knows what he wants	22	24	20
Because Adenauer was unable to arrange for Etzel to be his successor	21	26	16
Because Adenauer wants to take part in the Bundes- tag election campaign in 1961, which he cannot do as Federal President	19	20	19
Because Adenauer did not want Erhard to become Federal Chancellor	18	24	12
Because during his visit to America, President Eisenhower asked him to remain Chancellor . .	16	21	11
Because the Geneva conference has shown that the Western powers would give way to the Russians too much, if a weaker man than Adenauer represented the interests of West Germany	15	13	16
Other answers	2	2	2
Don't know	6	4	8
Remainder not questioned	9	5	13
Total	226	253	202

Question: "Do you think that Adenauer, in making his decisions, acted in accordance with the best of his knowledge and the dictates of his conscience, or was it more caprice, a decision made on the spur of the moment?"

June 1959

	Best of knowledge and conscience	Caprice, spur of the moment	Undecided, don't know	Heard nothing of Adenauer's decision	Total
	%	%	%	%	%
Total population . . .	42	22	27	9	= 100
Men	44	28	23	5	= 100
Women	41	16	30	13	= 100
CDU/CSU supporters	70	8	16	6	= 100
SPD supporters . . .	23	48	20	9	= 100

Question: "Do you think that it speaks for or against Adenauer that he changed his decision?"

June 1959

	Total population	Men	Women	Supporters: CDU/CSU	SPD
	%	%	%	%	%
Speaks against him .	46	57	37	28	67
Speaks for him . . .	14	15	13	28	7
Undecided, don't know	31	23	37	38	17
Heard nothing of Adenauer's decision	9	5	13	6	9
Total	100	100	100	100	100

Question: "Do you think that Adenauer's decision to remain Chancellor has improved or impaired our position in relation to the Western powers, or has nothing been changed?"

June 1959

A	Nothing changed	Im-paired	Im-proved	Don't know	Nothing known of Ade-auer's decision	Total
	%	%	%	%	%	%
Total population . . .	38	24	6	23	9	= 100
Men	43	29	6	17	5	= 100
Women	34	19	5	29	13	= 100
CDU/CSU supporters	50	13	12	19	6	= 100
SPD supporters . . .	28	37	3	23	9	= 100
FDP/DVP supporters .	58	31	×	11	×	= 100

Question: "Do you think that Adenauer's decision to remain Chancellor has improved or impaired our position in relation to Russia, or has nothing been changed?"

June 1959

A	Nothing changed	Im-paired	Im-proved	Don't know	Nothing known of Ade-nauers' decision	Total
	%	%	%	%	%	%
Total population . . .	41	19	7	24	9	= 100
Men	48	25	9	13	5	= 100
Women	35	15	4	33	13	= 100
CDU/CSU supporters	54	8	11	21	6	= 100
SPD supporters . . .	32	42	1	16	9	= 100
FDP/DVP supporters .	46	27	7	20	×	= 100

Question: "After Adenauer announced his decision to remain Federal Chancellor, people in Bonn considered whether they ought to depose Adenauer in such a manner that his own party would provide a different Federal Chancellor and remove Adenauer. Have you heard anything about this?"

July 1959

A	Yes	No	Remainder not questioned	Total
	%	%	%	%
Total population . .	53	40	7	= 100
Men	65	31	4	= 100
Women	44	46	10	= 100

Question: "If you had anything to say about it, should the CDU have removed Adenauer or not?"

July 1959

A	Removed	Not removed	Undecided, don't care	Remainder not questioned	Total
	%	%	%	%	%
Total population . .	40	29	24	7	= 100
Men	52	27	17	4	= 100
Women	29	32	29	10	= 100

Question: "Have you heard about the dispute between Adenauer and Erhard?"

July 1959

A	Yes, heard about it %	No, heard nothing %	Total %
Total population	87	13	= 100
Men	95	5	= 100
Women.	80	20	= 100

Question: "And how do you feel the dispute ended: Have Adenauer and Erhard completely settled their differences in the meantime, or are they now opposed to each other?"

July 1959

A	Opposed %	Differences settled %	Undecided %	Adenauer-Erhard dispute unknown %	Total %
Total population . .	33	25	29	13	= 100
Men	43	23	29	5	= 100
Women	24	27	29	20	= 100

Question: "Some people say: 'Even if Adenauer is convinced that Erhard would not have made a good Federal Chancellor, he should not have made the dispute public property.' On the other hand, others say: 'Erhard should not be so sensitive. After all, if Adenauer is asked, he can express his opinion openly.' — What do you think about it?"

July 1959

A	Not make dispute public	Express opinion openly	Undecided, no opinion	Adenauer-Erhard dispute unknown	Total
	%	%	%	%	%
Total population . .	50	22	15	13	= 100
Men	55	28	12	5	= 100
Women	44	18	18	20	= 100

Question: "Adenauer has said that Erhard has not sufficient experience in foreign affairs as yet for the office of Federal Chancellor. Erhard denies this and says he has gained enough experience in the past ten years to take over the political leadership. Which of them, in your opinion, is right?"

July 1959

A	Erhard	Adenauer	Undecided	Adenauer-Erhard dispute unknown	Total
	%	%	%	%	%
Total population . .	47	12	28	13	= 100
Men	58	12	25	5	= 100
Women	37	11	32	20	= 100

INTERNATIONAL RELATIONS

VI

The efforts of Adenauer to establish close relations of mutual trust with the powers of the free world has been watched carefully and unwaveringly supported by the German public.

Question: "Do you regard Adenauer's efforts to achieve good relations with France as right or wrong?"

November 1951

	Right	With re-servations, in favour	Wrong	Undecided, don't know	Total
	%	%	%	%	%
Total population . .	65	10	10	15	= 100
Men	68	14	13	5	= 100
Women	63	7	7	23	= 100
CDU/CSU supporters	75	7	7	11	= 100
SPD supporters . . .	64	12	14	10	= 100
FDP/DVP supporters .	74	13	8	5	= 100

Question: "What is your opinion: Did Adenauer's visit to America benefit Germany in any way?"

	Yes %	No %	Undecided %	No opinion %	Total %
Total population . .	47	12	15	26	= 100
Men	56	13	15	16	= 100
Women	40	9	16	35	= 100

Question: "Some time ago, the Federal Chancellor was in Greece and Turkey. What is your opinion: Did Adenauer's visits to Greece and Turkey benefit Germany in any way?"

(North Rhine-Westphalia)   *May 1954*

	Yes %	No %	No opinion %	Total %
Total population . .	42	16	42	= 100
Men	52	20	28	= 100
Women	34	12	54	= 100

Question: "The Russian government has invited Adenauer to Moscow. What is your opinion: Should Adenauer accept this invitation or refuse it?"

June 1955

	Should accept	Should not accept	Undecided	Don't know	Total
	%	%	%	%	%
Total population ..	82	3	6	9	= 100
Men	92	3	3	2	= 100
Women	73	4	8	15	= 100
CDU/CSU supporters	85	5	6	4	= 100
SPD supporters . . .	89	3	4	4	= 100

Question: "Have you heard that Adenauer recently visited President de Gaulle in France?"

December 1959

	Yes	No	Total
	%	%	%
Total population	85	15	= 100
Men	92	8	= 100
Women	79	21	= 100
CDU/CSU supporters	88	12	= 100
SPD supporters	88	12	= 100
FDP/DVP supporters	89	11	= 100

Question: "What is your opinion: Did Adenauer's visit to President de Gaulle benefit Germany in any way?"

December 1959

A	Yes	No	Un-decided	No opinion	Heard nothing about it	Total
	%	%	%	%	%	%
Total population . .	30	13	19	23	15	= 100
Men	38	16	20	18	8	= 100
Women	25	9	18	27	21	= 100
16—29 years old . .	29	9	18	26	18	= 100
30—44	29	16	20	25	10	= 100
45—59	32	14	17	20	17	= 100
60 and over	33	11	21	19	16	= 100
Primary school . . .	28	12	19	24	17	= 100
Secondary school . .	44	18	17	16	5	= 100
CDU/CSU supporters	42	6	17	23	12	= 100
SPD supporters . . .	28	21	22	17	12	= 100
FDP/DVP supporters .	31	29	9	20	11	= 100

Question put to persons who had heard of Adenauer's meeting with President de Gaulle:
"What are your feelings when you hear that Adenauer and de Gaulle often meet: Do you think that is good for us or not?"

December 1959

A	Good	Not good	Un-decided	Heard nothing about it	Total
	%	%	%	%	%
Total population	43	9	33	15	= 100
Men	53	11	28	8	= 100
Women	35	8	36	21	= 100
16—29 years old	40	8	34	18	= 100
30—44	42	11	37	10	= 100
45—49	45	11	27	17	= 100
60 and over	44	8	32	16	= 100
Primary school	40	8	35	17	= 100
Secondary school	58	14	23	5	= 100
CDU/CSU supporters	55	4	29	12	= 100
SPD supporters	41	16	31	12	= 100
FDP/DVP supporters	59	18	12	11	= 100

Question: "Have you heard that Adenauer recently visited Mr. Macmillan in England?"

December 1959

	Yes %	No %	Total %
Total population	79	21	= 100
Men	88	12	= 100
Women	69	31	= 100
CDU/CSU supporters	81	19	= 100
SPD supporters	85	15	= 100
FDP/DVP supporters	84	16	= 100

Question put to persons who had heard of Adenauer's visit to England: "What is your impression: Do you think that Adenauer's visit to Mr. Macmillan improved our relations to Britain or not?"

December 1959

A	Im-proved	Not im-proved	Unde-cided	Don't know	Heard nothing about it	Total
	%	%	%	%	%	%
Total population . .	37	14	15	13	21	= 100
Men	46	19	16	7	12	= 100
Women	29	9	15	18	29	= 100
16—29 years old . .	30	13	15	15	27	= 100
30—44	40	16	16	12	16	= 100
45—59	36	16	18	13	17	= 100
60 and over	46	8	10	12	24	= 100
Primary school . . .	34	13	15	14	24	= 100
Secondary school . .	49	17	18	9	7	= 100
CSU/CDU supporters	51	7	11	12	19	= 100
SPD supporters . . .	34	19	19	13	15	= 100
FDP/DVP supporters .	44	14	12	14	16	= 100

Question: "Have you heard that Adenauer was recently in America?"

	1960 March	1961 April	1961 December
	%	%	%
Yes	94	58	94
No	6	42	6
Total	100	100	100

Question put to persons who had heard that Adenauer was recently in America:
"What is your opinion: was Adenauer's visit to America of any benefit to Germany?"

A	1960 March	1961 April	1961 December
	%	%	%
Of great benefit	7	7	6
Yes, of benefit	30	28	28
No, no benefit	13	3	15
Had detrimental effect	1	1	1
Undecided	21	7	23
No opinion	22	12	21
Remainder not questioned	6	42	6
Total	100	100	100

THE POLITICIAN

VII

The "most capable German politician," is what the population soon called Adenauer. Other labels were added to this one, faded into insignificance, and made way for still others.

Question: "Whom do you consider the most capable German politician at the present time?"

November 1951

	Total popu- lation %	Men %	Women %	Supporters: CDU/ CSU %	SPD %	FDP/ DVP %
Konrad Adenauer . .	19	23	15	42	10	27
Other CDU politicians	3	4	2	4	3	5
Kurt Schumacher . .	11	16	7	2	34	4
Carlo Schmid	2	3	2	2	4	1
Other SPD politicians	1	2	1	1	2	1
Theodor Heuss . . .	3	3	4	3	3	7
Franz Blücher	1	1	1	1	1	5
Other FDP politicians	×	1	×	×	×	4
SRP politicians . . .	1	1	×	×	×	×
Other parties, other persons	3	4	2	1	1	×
None	11	14	8	6	8	12
Don't know, undecided	45	28	58	38	34	34
Total	100	100	100	100	100	100

Question: "Whom do you consider the most capable German politician at the present time?"

December 1951

	Total population	Men	Women	Supporters: CDU/ CSU	SPD	FDP/ DVP
	%	%	%	%	%	%
Konrad Adenauer . .	26	29	22	56	11	46
Kurt Schumacher . .	13	18	8	5	43	5
Theodor Heuss . . .	3	3	3	1	6	7
Carlo Schmid	2	3	1	1	4	4
Franz Blücher	1	1	×	1	×	4
Others	6	10	3	6	4	9
None	12	14	9	5	8	7
Don't know, undecided	37	22	54	25	24	18
Total	100	100	100	100	100	100

Question: "Whom do you consider the most capable German politician at the present time?"

January 1952

	Total popu- lation	Men	Women	Supporters: CDU/ CSU	SPD	FDP/ DVP
	%	%	%	%	%	%
Konrad Adenauer . .	27	28	26	68	12	37
Kurt Schumacher . .	14	22	8	2	52	6
Theodor Heuss . . .	3	2	3	3	2	6
Carlo Schmid	2	2	1	1	4	1
Franz Blücher	×	×	×	×	×	1
Others	6	9	5	2	5	10
None	12	15	10	4	6	15
Don't know, undecided	36	22	47	20	19	24
Total	100	100	100	100	100	100

Question: "Whom do you consider the most capable German politician at the present time?"

August 1952

A	Total population	Men	Women	Supporters: CDU/ CSU	SPD	FDP/ DVP
	%	%	%	%	%	%
Konrad Adenauer . .	33	36	32	72	15	49
Kurt Schumacher . .	12	16	9	2	40	×
Theodor Heuss . . .	5	3	6	5	4	8
Carlo Schmid	3	4	2	×	7	5
Erich Ollenhauer . .	1	2	×	×	4	×
Franz Blücher	1	1	×	×	×	3
Hjalmar Schacht . . .	1	1	×	×	×	×
Other names	6	8	5	3	4	14
Don't know any. . .	9	9	8	3	6	6
Don't know, no (definite) answer . .	29	20	38	15	20	15
Total	100	100	100	100	100	100

Question: "Whom do you consider the most capable German politician at the present time?"

May/June 1953

	Total popu- lation	Men	Women	Age groups: 18 to 29	30 to 44	45 to 59	60 and over
	%	%	%	%	%	%	%
Konrad Adenauer . .	51	56	46	45	53	51	53
Erich Ollenhauer . .	6	10	4	6	7	6	6
Theodor Heuss . . .	3	2	3	3	2	1	4
Ernst Reuter	1	1	1	1	1	1	1
Carlo Schmid	1	2	1	1	1	2	1
Other names	5	8	2	5	5	7	3
Don't know any . .	6	7	5	6	8	6	5
Don't know, no (definite) answer. .	27	14	38	33	23	26	27
Total	100	100	100	100	100	100	100

Question: "Whom do you consider the most capable German politician at the present time?"

November 1953

A	Total population %	Men %	Women %	Supporters: CDU/ CSU %	SPD %	FDP/ DVP %
Konrad Adenauer . .	62	66	59	87	43	66
Other CDU politicians	1	2	1	1	1	5
Erich Ollenhauer . .	3	4	2	×	16	×
Other SPD politicians	1	1	×	×	3	×
Theodor Heuss . . .	2	2	2	1	2	3
Other FDP politicians	×	×	×	×	×	×
Other parties, other politicians . . .	1	2	1	×	×	2
Don't know any . .	6	8	4	1	9	6
Don't know, undecided	24	15	31	10	26	18
Total	100	100	100	100	100	100

Question: "Whom do you consider the most capable German politician at the present time?"

January 1955

A	Total popu-lation	Men	Women	Supporters: CDU/CSU	SPD	FDP/DVP
	%	%	%	%	%	%
Konrad Adenauer . .	55	59	51	86	31	67
Other CDU politicians	3	3	3	1	4	4
Erich Ollenhauer . .	6	7	4	×	21	×
Other SPD politicians	3	4	2	×	10	2
Theodor Heuss . . .	4	2	5	3	5	1
Other FDP politicians	1	2	1	×	1	7
Other parties, other politicians . . .	2	2	2	×	1	×
There are none . . .	4	6	3	1	7	1
Don't know, undecided	23	15	30	9	21	19
Total	101	100	101	100	101	101

Question: "Whom do you consider the most capable German politician at the present time?"

January 1956

A	Total population %	Men %	Women %	Supporters: CDU/ CSU %	SPD %	FDP/ DVP %
Konrad Adenauer . .	56	57	55	82	42	68
Other CDU politicians	4	6	3	5	4	4
Erich Ollenhauer . .	6	8	4	×	22	×
Other SPD politicians	3	5	2	2	8	1
Theodor Heuss . . .	2	2	3	2	2	4
Other FDP politicians	3	4	1	×	3	9
Other parties, other politicians . . .	×	1	×	×	1	×
There are none . . .	5	7	3	×	6	4
Don't know, undecided	22	12	30	10	14	10
Total	101	102	101	101	102	100

Question: "Whom do you consider the most capable German politician at the present time?"

September 1957

	Total population %	Men %	Women %	Primary school %	Secondary school %
Konrad Adenauer	45	46	45	43	51
Other CDU politicians	7	9	4	6	9
Erich Ollenhauer	8	10	5	9	3
Other SPD politicians	4	8	2	5	3
Theodor Heuss	1	1	1	1	2
Other FDP politicians	1	1	1	1	1
Other parties, other politicians	1	1	×	1	2
There are none	3	4	3	3	4
Don't know, undecided . . .	30	20	39	31	25
Total	100	100	100	100	100

Question: "Whom do you consider the most capable German politician at the present time?"

August 1961

| | Total population | Men | Women | Supporters: ([2]) | | |
				CDU/ CSU	SPD	FDP/ DVP
	%	%	%	%	%	%
Konrad Adenauer . .	26	23	28	57	7	16
Other CDU politicians	23	28	18	28	11	45
Willy Brandt	21	24	19	3	54	5
Other SPD politicians .	5	8	3	1	13	2
Theodor Heuss . . .	1	1	1	1	1	1
Other FDP politicians	2	3	2	1	1	14
Other parties, other politicians . . .	×	×	×	×	×	×
There are none . . .	2	3	2	1	2	3
Don't know, undecided	22	14	29	12	15	17
Total	102	104	102	104	104	103

Question: "If you look through this list, who, in your opinion, is the most capable politician we have in Germany at the present time?" (L)

June 1959

	Total popu-lation	Men	Women	Supporters: CDU/ CSU	SPD	FDP/ DVP
	%	%	%	%	%	%
Konrad Adenauer . .	28	27	29	54	10	13
Willy Brandt	17	20	15	8	28	18
Ludwig Erhard . . .	13	15	11	13	9	25
Theodor Heuss . . .	10	8	12	8	11	9
Carlo Schmid	9	12	6	2	22	11
Erich Ollenhauer . .	3	4	3	1	9	×
Eugen Gerstenmaier .	3	4	3	2	3	10
Heinrich Lübke . . .	2	2	2	2	1	1
Heinrich von Brentano	1	1	1	1	1	3
Heinrich Krone . . .	1	1	×	1	×	×
Franz Etzel	×	×	×	×	×	3
Fritz Schäfer.	×	×	×	×	×	×
Karl Mommer . . .	×	×	×	×	×	×
Gerhard Schröder . .	×	×	×	×	×	×
Franz-Josef Strauß . .	×	×	×	1	×	×
Others	×	×	×	×	1	×
Don't know, no (definite) answer . .	15	9	19	8	8	10
Total	102	103	101	101	103	103

Question: "Which living politician do you esteem most?"

September 1959

	Total popu-lation %	Men %	Women %	Supporters: CDU/CSU %	SPD %	FDP/DVP %
Theodor Heuss . . .	28	27	29	22	31	44
Konrad Adenauer . .	27	24	31	55	9	15
Ludwig Erhard . . .	9	13	6	10	14	18
Willy Brandt	7	8	6	3	16	3
Erich Ollenhauer . .	3	5	2	×	11	2
Carlo Schmid	4	6	2	1	12	×
Others	5	6	4	4	5	8
Don't esteem any of them	8	8	8	3	4	5
Don't know	14	10	17	8	9	7
Total	105	107	105	106	111	102

THE GREAT NAME

VIII

When Adenauer became prominent in post-war history, first as President of the Constituent Assembly, then as head of the Government, there were sensitive people who feared the reawakening of nationalistic tendencies directed against him, the democrat; the gradual genesis of a Hitler myth was in the air. At that time, still under the shadow of denazification, there were approximately 10 per cent who regarded Hitler as the "great German", who had "done most for Germany". So his name was placed immediately after that of Bismarck — Adenauer was not mentioned at all in that poll. This chapter clearly shows how the appearance of a great man on the scene can influence and alter the conception of history in his epoch. In less than a decade, public opinion put Adenauer at the top of the list of "great Germans", above Bismarck — to say nothing of Hitler, who no longer polled even 5 per cent.

Perhaps another politician from the right or left wing would also have had the will, strength, ability and personality to destroy the nimbus of the so-called "Third Reich" by a successful policy based on the freedom and dignity of the individual. But in his era, it was Adenauer who performed this great work.

Question: "In your opinion, which great German has done most for Germany?"

January 1950

	%
Bismarck	35
Hitler	10
Fredrick the Great	7
Hindenburg	6
Goethe	4
William II	3
Martin Luther	3
Baron vom Stein	2
William I	2
Charlemagne	2
Stresemann	2
Robert Koch	2
Brüning	2
Ebert	1
Karl Marx	1
57 other names	6
None, don't know	15
Total	103

Question: "In your opinion, which great German has done most for Germany?"

August 1952

A	Total popu- lation	Men	Women	Supporters: CDU/ CSU	SPD	FDP/ DVP
	%	%	%	%	%	%
Bismarck	36	43	31	36	34	61
Hitler	9	8	10	4	8	7
Hindenburg	7	6	7	8	6	6
Fredrick the Great . .	7	7	7	8	6	7
Kaisers, kings, generals, soldiers . . .	7	7	8	8	9	6
Adenauer	3	2	3	6	1	5
Democratic and liberal politicians	5	5	4	5	11	1
Goethe	3	3	3	3	3	6
Authors, artists, philosophers	3	3	4	3	4	3
Scientists, inventors .	3	4	2	2	2	×
Others	2	3	1	2	2	×
Don't know, no answer	18	13	22	16	18	2
Total	103	104	102	101	104	104

Question: "In your opinion, which great German has done most for Germany?"

November 1953

A	Total popu-lation	Men	Women	CDU/ CSU	Supporters: SPD	FDP/ DVP
	%	%	%	%	%	%
Bismarck	32	40	25	35	32	52
Adenauer	9	8	10	18	2	7
Hitler	9	10	9	5	8	7
Fredrick the Great . .	6	7	5	4	5	12
Kaisers, kings, generals, soldiers . . .	10	8	12	9	8	12
Democratic and liberal politicians	3	5	2	2	10	3
Authors, artists, philosophers	4	4	5	7	2	1
Scientists, inventors .	3	3	3	3	5	1
Others	4	4	4	4	3	5
Don't know, no answer	24	18	30	20	27	7
Total	104	107	105	107	102	107

Question: "If you compare Adenauer with Bismarck, who, do you think, is the greater statesman?"

December 1954

	Bismarck	Adenauer	Other answers	No opinion	Total
	%	%	%	%	%
Total population . .	52	11	4	33	= 100
Men	59	10	5	26	= 100
Women	47	12	3	38	= 100
18—29 years old . .	46	12	2	40	= 100
30—44	54	12	3	31	= 100
45—59	52	11	4	33	= 100
60 and over	58	9	7	26	= 100
Primary school . . .	53	10	3	34	= 100
Secondary school . .	50	16	6	28	= 100
Secondary school graduates ("Abitur") .	50	12	4	34	= 100
Workers.	53	10	3	34	= 100
Agriculture	47	11	3	39	= 100
Others	53	12	7	28	= 100
Protestants	58	10	3	29	= 100
Catholics	43	14	5	38	= 100
Others, including those of no religious denomination	59	4	2	35	= 100
North Germany . . .	61	6	3	30	= 100
West Germany. . . .	47	14	5	34	= 100
South Germany . . .	54	11	3	32	= 100
West Berlin	40	15	×	45	= 100
CDU/CSU supporters	36	23	6	35	= 100
SPD supporters . . .	68	6	3	23	= 100
FDP/DVP supporters .	65	7	7	21	= 100
BHE supporters . . .	62	9	4	25	= 100

Question: "If you compare Adenauer with Hitler, who, do you think, is the greater statesman?"

December 1954

	Adenauer	Hitler	Other answers	No opinion	Total
	%	%	%	%	%
Total population . .	49	14	7	30	= 100
Men	53	16	8	23	= 100
Women	47	12	5	36	= 100
18—29 years old . .	45	18	4	33	= 100
30—44	50	13	8	29	= 100
45—59	46	14	9	31	= 100
60 and over	59	10	4	27	= 100
Primary school . . .	47	14	6	33	= 100
Secondary school . .	56	15	6	23	= 100
Secondary school graduates ("Abitur") .	68	6	9	17	= 100
Workers.	45	16	8	31	= 100
Agriculture	43	11	4	42	= 100
Others	58	12	6	24	= 100
Protestants	46	15	7	32	= 100
Catholics	54	11	7	28	= 100
Others, including those of not religious denomination	48	18	8	26	= 100
North Germany . . .	39	16	11	34	= 100
West Germany. . . .	48	17	5	30	= 100
South Germany . . .	54	11	7	28	= 100
West Berlin	72	4	4	20	= 100
CDU/CSU supporters	72	5	2	21	= 100
SPD supporters . . .	41	16	13	30	= 100
FDP/DVP supporters .	58	21	7	14	= 100
BHE supporters . . .	52	12	9	27	= 100

Question: "In your opinion, which great German has done most for Germany?"

January 1955

A	Total popu- lation	Men	Women	Supporters: CDU/ CSU	SPD	FDP/ DVP
	%	%	%	%	%	%
Bismarck	30	34	28	27	28	43
Adenauer	17	15	19	32	9	10
Hitler	7	8	6	3	7	3
Fredrick the Great . .	4	4	3	3	6	8
Kaisers, kings, generals, soldiers . . .	11	11	12	10	14	8
Democratic and liberal politicians	7	9	4	4	14	8
Authors, artists, philosophers	5	5	5	2	6	9
Scientists, inventors .	3	3	3	3	4	4
Others	2	3	2	3	1	4
Don't know, no answer	17	10	21	14	13	8
Total	103	102	103	101	102	105

Question: "In your opinion, which great German has done most for Germany?"

September 1955

A	Total popu-lation	Men	Women	Supporters: CDU/CSU	SPD	FDP/DVP
	%	%	%	%	%	%
Bismarck	32	37	28	31	28	48
Adenauer	15	14	15	30	3	8
Fredrick the Great . .	6	7	5	5	6	9
Hitler	6	7	5	5	6	8
Kaisers, kings, generals, soldiers . . .	11	11	11	8	13	8
Democratic and liberal politicians	6	8	5	3	16	3
Authors, artists, philosophers	7	5	8	5	9	11
Scientists, inventors .	4	5	4	3	6	6
Others	2	2	2	1	2	2
Don't know, no answer	17	10	24	15	16	6
Total	106	106	107	106	105	109

Question: "In your opinion, which great German has done most for Germany?"

January 1956

A	Total population	Men	Women	Supporters: CDU/ CSU	SPD	FDP/ DVP
	%	%	%	%	%	%
Bismarck	27	37	20	23	22	50
Adenauer	24	21	27	45	14	17
Hitler.	8	7	9	4	9	5
Fredrick the Great	3	3	3	3	4	1
Kaisers, kings, generals, soldiers	7	7	8	6	10	5
Democratic and liberal politicians	7	9	5	3	18	7
Authors, artists, philosophers .	4	4	4	5	2	7
Scientists, inventors	2	2	2	3	3	2
Others	3	1	4	3	2	3
Don't know, undecided . .	18	13	21	9	19	9
Total	103	104	103	104	103	106

Question: "In your opinion, which great German has done most for Germany?"

October 1958

A	Total popu-lation %	Men %	Women %	Supporters: CDU/ CSU %	SPD %	FDP/ DVP %
Adenauer	26	21	30	48	13	9
Bismarck	23	32	16	23	23	35
Fredrick the Great . .	2	2	2	1	2	2
Hitler	4	4	4	2	4	9
Kaisers, kings, generals, soldiers . . .	7	6	7	5	9	7
Democratic and liberal politicians	10	12	8	3	22	5
Authors, artists, philosophers	4	3	4	3	4	7
Scientists, inventors .	3	3	2	3	2	9
Others	1	2	1	×	2	5
Don't know, undecided	21	16	26	12	19	14
Total	101	101	100	100	100	102

147

Question: "In your opinion, which great German has done most for Germany?"

	1950 Jan.	1952 Aug.	1953 Nov.	1955 Jan.	1955 Sept.	1958 Oct.
	%	%	%	%	%	%
Bismarck	35	36	32	30	32	23
Adenauer	—	3	9	17	15	26
Hitler	10	9	9	7	6	4

Question: "Where would you place this man: Would you count Adenauer among the really great men of our century, or wouldn't you rate him as so significant?"

May 1958

	Among really great %	Not so significant %	Undecided, no opinion %	Total %
Total population	53	27	20	= 100
Men	55	33	12	= 100
Women	51	22	27	= 100
Primary school	50	28	22	= 100
Secondary school	65	23	12	= 100
CDU/CSU supporters . .	79	10	11	= 100
SPD supporters	34	50	16	= 100
FDP/DVP supporters . . .	48	38	14	= 100

APPENDIX

PERCENTAGES — This book contains tables in which the percentage figures add up to more than 100. Such results are obtained in the case of questions to which more than one answer could be given.

Where only one answer could be given to a question because the various answers were mutually exclusive, the addition of the percentage figures always produces a total of 100.

Where less than 0.5 per cent of respondents selected any answer, an "x" is entered in the tables instead of a figure.

EDUCATION LEVEL — "Primary school" denotes completion of education at a "Volksschule" (normally eight years elementary schooling) or training at a secondary school to a level not above the tenth class (grade) (approx. 82 per cent of population). The "secondary school" group includes persons whose schooling was terminated on obtaining a "school-leaving certificate" ("Mittlere Reife") after successful completion of tenth class (grade) studies (approx. 14 per cent of population). "Secondary school graduates" are persons who normally complete 12 to 13 years secondary education and pass the final ("Abitur" = matriculation) examination entitling them to study at a university (approx. 4 per cent of population).

OCCUPATIONAL GROUPS — In some tables the poll results are classified according to occupation groups. Such groups include both persons engaged in those occupations and the members of their families. For example, "workers" include not only the employed workers, but also the members of their families.

The term "agriculture" comprises farmers and agricultural workers.

SYMBOLS — Tables not marked by any symbol contain results of statistically representative public opinion polls of the Institut für Demoskopie Allensbach, each based on 2,000 oral interviews with persons aged 16 or over in the territory of the German Federal Republic and West Berlin.

Tables marked with an "A" contain results of polls of 1,000 persons in the territory of the German Federal Republic and West Berlin.

Tables in which the text of the question is marked with an "L" are based on interviews in which a list of answers was submitted for the respondents to choose from.

Tables in which the text of the question is marked with a "K" are based on interviews in which a pack of cards with a large number of answers was submitted to respondents.

Tables in which the text of the question is marked with a "B" are based on interviews in which respondents were presented with an illustrated sheet.

NOTES — (1) In the first poll in 1951, the term "chief objection" was used, while in the subsequent polls only the word "objection" was employed.

(2) Only electors in German Federal Republic excluding West-Berlin.